· REDISCOVERING RAILWAYS ·

NORFOLK

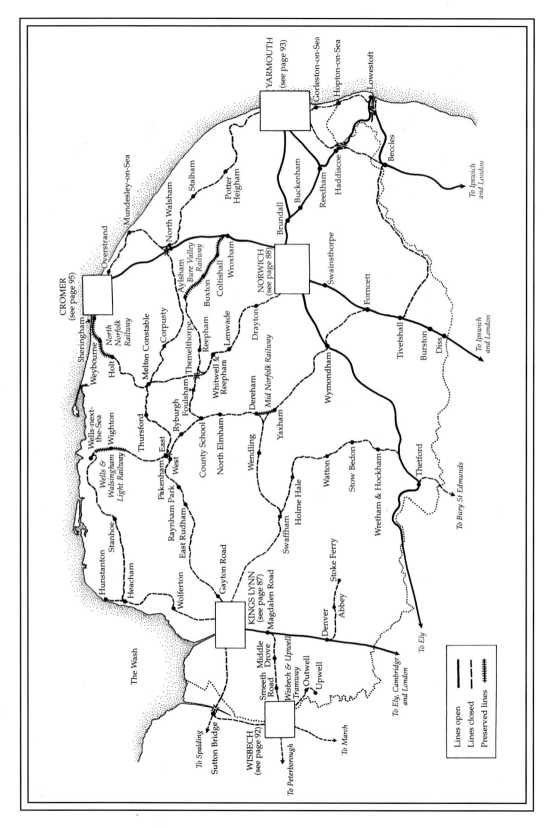

Map of the railways of Norfolk, showing principal locations and others illustrated in the book.

· REDISCOVERING RAILWAYS ·

NORFOLK

A pictorial record of the county's railways past and present

Des Saunders
and
Richard Adderson

· RAILWAY HERITAGE ·
from
The NOSTALGIA *Collection*

First published in 1999
Reprinted 2005

British Library Cataloguing in Publication Data

A catalogue record for this book is available from the British Library.

ISBN 1 85895 144 5

Past & Present Publishing Ltd
The Trundle
Ringstead Road
Great Addington
Kettering
Northants
NN14 4BW

Tel/Fax: 01536 330588
email: sales@nostalgiacollection.com
Website: www.nostalgiacollection.com

Much of the material in this book first appeared in *British Railways Past and Present, No 12 East Anglia*, by the same authors and published by Past & Present Publishing Ltd in 1991.

Main map drawn by Christina Siviter; Gazetteer maps drawn by Geoffrey Body

Printed and bound in Great Britain

Past and Present

A Past & Present book
from
*The **NOSTALGIA** Collection*

MAGDALEN ROAD (now named WATLINGTON) represents a welcome revival in the fortunes of Norfolk's railways. In the 'past' picture a 'J19' Class 0-6-0 locomotive shunts the pick-up goods in the yard, having left some of its wagons on the down main line. The main line to Ely disappears straight head into the Fenland mists, while the branch to Wisbech and March curves away behind the platelayers hut.

CONTENTS

In the 'present' equivalent a Cambridge-bound DMU has discharged a handful of passengers, but then it was market day down the line in Kings Lynn. The wires are up, ready for electrification of the service. The station closed in 1968, but re-opened seven years later; it is now named Watlington, although the signal box stubbornly remains Magdalen Road. On the right a van is parked on the trackbed of the Wisbech line, and a short length of the goods platform can clearly be seen; on the left a small estate of houses has sprung up. *Norfolk Railway Society Archive/DGS*

STOW BEDON: It was perhaps surprising that the very rural line from Thetford to Swaffham lasted as long as it did, but it could not survive the Beeching Report, closing in June 1964, although a limited goods service from Swaffham to Watton lingered on until April 1965. On 13 June 1964, the last day of passenger services, the 2.25 from Swaffham runs over the level crossing to pick up its single passenger at Stow Bedon.

Nothing much is left here today; one has to depend on an Ordnance Survey map, preferably an old one. The old station yard is now the entrance to the circular Pingles walk of some 8 miles, utilising part of the Peddars Way and returning via the old trackbed. The massive concrete post of the level crossing gate is the only clue that a railway once ran here; the rest of the site is a wilderness, while across the road is a dwelling house, formerly a pub. Nature-lovers may be interested to know that the Great Eastern Pingle Trail project was opened by Norfolk County Council in conjunction with the Countryside Commission, the Norfolk Naturalists Trust and the Manpower Services Commission, and the part along the old line is particularly noted for its diversity of butterflies. *RJA/DGS*

INTRODUCTION

You cannot travel far in Norfolk without coming across the tell-tale remains of former railway lines – a line of post-and-wire fencing enclosing an area of scrubland for no apparent reason, or the brick abutments of a demolished bridge by a neglected and overgrown embankment. Our tour of Norfolk will reveal that the county, being essentially a rural area, has suffered more than most from railway closures, but at the time of writing the surviving lines appear to have a secure future. Fast and frequent electric trains link both Kings Lynn and Norwich with London, while other express services connect Norwich with the Midlands and North. By contrast, local trains on the lines from Norwich to the coast still serve their market towns and rural communities as they have done for well over a century.

A glance at the map will show how the railways criss-crossed the county. It was here in Norfolk that the old Great Eastern Railway had its only real competition. This came in the form of the Midland & Great Northern Joint Railway, running across the county from Yarmouth to Kings Lynn and ultimately on to Peterborough and the Midlands, with branches to the North Norfolk coast and the county capital. As a result, towns such as North Walsham, Aylsham and Fakenham were able to boast two railway stations. The 'Joint', as it became known, handled heavy traffic over largely single track in its heyday, but with the exception of the Cromer branch and one or two freight spurs, its 182 route miles were closed completely on 28 February 1959. It was the first major railway closure in the country.

The scale of the M&GN closure was a shock at the time, as previous service withdrawals had affected only little-used rural branch lines. In the west the line from Stoke Ferry to Denver had lost its passenger services as long ago as 1930, while in the early 1950s the last passenger trains had run on the coastal lines from Heacham to Wells and from Mundesley to Cromer, and on the cross-country branch from County School to Wroxham. The pace of railway closures was to increase rapidly during the early 1960s following the infamous Beeching report, removing centres like Swaffham, Fakenham and Watton from the timetables.

It was against this background that we set out, armed with a selection of old photographs, to discover how the railway scene in Norfolk had changed over the years. In the 1950s and 1960s, when many of the 'past' photographs in this book were taken, there was of course considerable variety in the railway scene, and it was this variety that was the attraction to many enthusiasts of the era. With trains likely to be formed of a rich selection of rolling-stock anything up to 40 years old, and to be hauled by any one of a number of locomotive classes, there was a sense of anticipation to see what would actually turn up. On the other hand, there was an air of permanence about the stations, where in many cases ancient lamps and signs dating back to pre-Grouping days lasted well into the 1950s.

By and large it is the opposite that applies today, as there is an unprecedented degree of uniformity and predictability in the trains themselves. To us, while visiting locations for the book, the uncertainty and anticipation was not about the type of train we would see, but more about how the location had changed. Would it be possible to find a similar viewpoint to yesteryear? Would any of yesteryear's features still be there, or would 'bus shelter'-type buildings and the overhead catenary have removed all traces? In many cases, of course, we knew we would not see a railway, and here the question was even more basic – would there be anything to see at all, or would a road improvement scheme, industrial estate, or indeed a return to nature have obliterated the site entirely? Frustratingly it sometimes proved impossible to duplicate the original viewpoint. However, when we were able to find features to link the photographs, whether obvious or not, our sense of satisfaction was no less than it would have been if, in the old days, a 'J15' and two ancient coaches had appeared instead of the expected diesel railcar.

We found that the production of an old photograph was a key that opened many doors. The majority of owner-occupiers were only too happy to show us around, point out remaining memorabilia, and show, in their opinion, the exact spot from which the previous photograph was taken. Present-day railwaymen were for the most part also very interested, the older men particularly wallowing in nostalgia.

The welcome was sometimes rather guarded, however. While one of us was taking photographs at the old Lenwade station he was accompanied for some 300 yards along the trackbed by a very unfriendly alsatian, barking loudly, and separated from him only by what appeared to be a rather flimsy wire fence. The photographer was hoping that the fence would hold. The dog obviously hoped otherwise. . .

Des Saunders
Mattishall

Richard Adderson
Norwich

A different variation on the 'past and present' theme: tickets from the M&GN, Great Eastern and British Railways eras compared with the tickets issued on the same lines in the 1990s. *RJA*

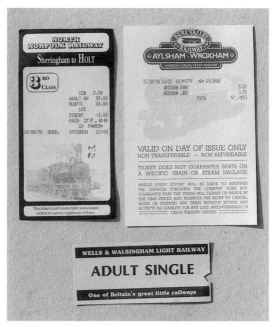

WEST NORFOLK

Kings Lynn and Hunstanton

ABBEY: In October 1965 Abbey station, on the Stoke Ferry branch, was still neat and tidy although it had lost its original canopy, following the withdrawal of the passenger service in 1930. It remained in use as the junction for the Wissington Light Railway, serving a sugar beet factory, until the early 1980s, although the line on to Stoke Ferry had closed completely in April 1965. One of the Wissington Railway steam locos can be seen at the platform end; during the sugar beet season long freight trains were commonplace.

This sparsely populated area was never going to make a profit for a railway and today only a short length of platform remains and a small corrugated hut on the platform. Just out of sight, the crossing keeper's cottage and station master's house appear to be in good order and in private occupation; a notice proclaims 'Trials Moto X Circuit, Station Farm', and a telephone number. *RJA/DGS*

STOKE FERRY: As already noted, passenger services on the branch from Denver were early victims of the LNER's economy drive, being withdrawn in 1930. Occasional goods trains continued to run until 1965, but this was almost certainly the final visit of a passenger train to the terminus. Class '4MT' 2-6-0 No 43149, having made a welcome return visit to its former M&GN haunts at East Rudham earlier in the day, pulls in with a special on 26 May 1962.

In 1991 the station house is occupied and in a good state of repair, whilst a timber firm occupies the track area. Had passenger receipts been greater the line would have been extended to the small village of Gooderstone, but in the event the proposed extension would have done nothing to lengthen the life of the branch. *Both RJA*

MIDDLE DROVE: The line from Magdalen Road across the flat fenland to Wisbech opened as early as 1848. Middle Drove was the first station on the branch, and its rather basic facilities are seen here as a 'J17' 0-6-0 rumbles through with an ancient van in tow.

Another lonely spot, seen on a dreary autumn afternoon, but station house and shelter on the down side are still intact, the platform sloping away into a ploughed field. 'It will cost you 50p,' said the young lady coming out of the station house. 'Dad would like a chat about the station. I'll get him.' But unfortunately Dad did not emerge.
D. Thompson/DGS

SMEETH ROAD: Taken at around the time of nationalisation, this study of Smeeth Road typifies the rural branch-line station, and with only detail differences could have been taken at any time during the previous 30 years.

When I visited the former station in the autumn of 1990, the owner of the signal box and waiting room (known as 'Annie's room' in this part of the world) was delighted when I showed him the photograph of the station taken some 30 years before, and immediately offered to buy it from me. We settled for swapping addresses. He then showed us a Midland six-wheel coach splendidly converted to a cosy office; he has plans to convert the signal box to a hairdressing salon – surely a first – while the 18-lever frame, still in situ, is going to the Nene Valley Railway. Apparently it was a rule that all signal boxes in this area had a Bible kept in them. *D. Thompson/DGS*

OUTWELL (WISBECH & UPWELL TRAMWAY): The Wisbech & Upwell Tramway served its agricultural community well enough for some 80 years after the first train ran in 1882. Although passenger services were withdrawn in 1928, the goods service soldiered on until 1966, by which time the original steam tram engines had been replaced by diesel shunters. Here one of the tram locos, the inspiration for Rev Awdry's 'Toby', provides entertainment for the village children at Outwell in the very early days.

Becoming more and more of an anachronism with each passing year, the tramway eventually closed in May 1966, and the tracks were removed a few years later. Few traces of the line remained in 1991, but the houses on the left were much the same and the two houses in the distance remained, and although the trains may have stopped, the canal beyond still flows. *A. C. Ingram/DGS*

KINGS LYNN: Days of transition at Kings Lynn – 'B12/3' 4-6-0 No 61514 runs into the station with a long parcels train on 6 August 1959 while two other steam locos darken the sky outside the loco shed on the left. The presence of Brush Type 2 diesel No D5534 standing alongside the signal box is an indication of things to come.

Thirty-two years later transition is again in the air, and the diesels are on their way out as Kings Lynn station waits for the electric era to begin. With the overhead wiring in place, a three-car Class '101' diesel multiple unit (DMU) heads for Cambridge over much reduced trackwork. The box and the fine signal gantries have been gone for many years, while the loco shed area is now the station car park.

The electric service began in 1992, and here we see a representative of the new order, unit No 365520, arriving on a West Anglia Great Northern Railway service from Kings Cross on 25 April 1998. The platform has been extended and new lighting installed. *A. E. Bennett/RJA (2)*

G. E. R.

From _____

TO

KING'S LYNN

KINGS LYNN DOCKS: After a shunting turn in the docks, 0-6-0 diesel No 08665 heads back to Kings Lynn yard on 9 October 1984.

Rail traffic over the branch to the docks ceased in the early 1990s, although there is hope of a revival. Undergrowth has spread across the track, and when the site was revisited on 25 April 1998 it was impossible to tell whether or not the rails were still in place. *Both RJA*

WOLFERTON: On a bright winter morning in 1950 the Royal Train stands at Wolferton station on the Royal Estate awaiting King George VI and Queen Elizabeth, at the end of their traditional Christmas holiday at Sandringham. The loco is one of the 'Clauds' kept especially clean by Kings Lynn depot for Royal Train duties – a Cambridge 'Sandringham' Class 4-6-0 was maintained in a similar condition for the same purpose. Even after the run-down and closure of the Hunstanton line, royalty continued to travel as far as Kings Lynn by rail, often in a special coach attached to a normal service train, before finishing their journey to Sandringham by road. Royal patronage has ceased now that the Kings Lynn line is operated by outer suburban electric multiple units.

Following closure, the buildings on the up platform were converted to residential use, whilst for many years the down platform buildings housed a railway museum, with particular emphasis on Royal Train travel. As a result the ornate buildings remain in a good state of repair, and continue to blend well with their surroundings. *Eastern Daily Press/RJA*

HUNSTANTON: The railway from Kings Lynn reached Hunstanton in 1862, and the town grew rapidly from then on. Its station, right next to the sea, handled heavy traffic for a century, with regular through trains from London and summer excursions from the Midlands terminating at the two island platforms. Two 'D16/3' 4-4-0s, Nos 62524 (tender first) and 62597, wait at Hunstanton on 6 August 1959; this was something of a scoop for the photographer, as only 13 of this well-loved and once-numerous class still survived at that time. The air of prosperity, however, is misleading; less than a decade later the line had closed entirely, the last train running over the singled track into a forlorn terminus in May 1969.

Now the station area is a car park, with the flat-roofed building on the right, and the adjoining double chimney pots, providing a link between the two views. *A. E. Bennett/DGS*

MAIN LINES TO NORWICH, YARMOUTH AND CROMER

DISS: 'History begins yesterday', they say, and certainly this is the case at Diss. The northern approach to the station had a distinctly traditional look about it as recently as 1 September 1984, with complicated trackwork and even a 16-

ton mineral wagon standing on a grass-grown siding. Class '47' No 47587 is approaching with the 12.32 from Norwich to Liverpool Street.

Just seven years later the main line has been electrified and things have been tidied up considerably. The trackwork has been simplified, although the kink in the remaining siding remains from the earlier scene. The jumble of buildings in the goods yard has been swept away, and a 'pay and display' car park has replaced the previous haphazard parking amongst the huts. Class '86' No 86220 *Round Tabler* approaches the station with a typical up express of the 'nineties. *D. C. Pearce/RJA*

BURSTON: Following their introduction in 1958, the English Electric Type 4 diesels, later known as Class '40', began to oust the 'Britannia' 'Pacifics' from the Ipswich main line expresses. D206, however, is on a far more mundane duty as it pulls into Burston station with the 6.08 pm stopping train from Norwich to Ipswich on 27 June 1964. Only one of the four vehicles appears to have passenger accommodation, and the Gresley full brake at the front contrasts with the modern diesel.

In common with the other wayside village stations on the route, Burston closed in November 1966, and the platforms were later demolished. The station building, which replaced an older structure between the wars, is still used by a local furniture maker, and the different coloured brickwork reveals where the poster boards used to be. The main line has of course been electrified, and the area is now controlled by Colchester power box. *Both RJA*

TIVETSHALL: Until January 1953 passengers could change at Tivetshall for the Waveney Valley branch train to Beccles). Although both the branch and the station closed completely in 1966, the signal box, refuge loop and some of the sidings survived for another 20 years. No 47583 *County of Hertfordshire* passes the box with the 9.30 am from Liverpool Street to Norwich on 1 September 1984, while an engineers vehicle stands on the surviving stub of the Waveney Valley branch.

The whole line to Norwich is now controlled by Colchester power box, and Tivetshall box was demolished soon after becoming redundant; the sidings and loop were removed at the same time. With the inelegant DBSO leading, a down express passes the site of Tivetshall box in August 1991. The concrete ballast bin on the right has survived the changes, whilst a yellow BR van shows that the railway still has some interest in the former yard area.
D. C. Pearce/RJA

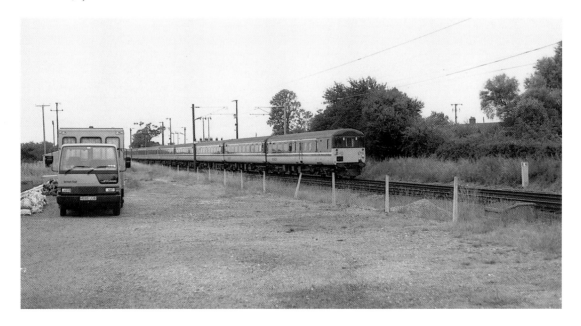

SWAINSTHORPE station closed in 1954, but the signal box remained in use until October 1986. It is still very much a traditional railway scene as Class '47' No 47542 passes a semaphore signal and approaches the box and level crossing gates with a down express on 29 June 1985. However, the newly erected electrification masts indicate that things are about to change.

And change they did! In May 1998 nature has taken over where the box once stood, a half-barrier crossing bars the way to road traffic, and a new wall precludes any more than a glimpse of the approaching train. *Both RJA*

The signal box, however, still survives, having been moved to the Wells terminus of the 10¼-inch-gauge Wells & Walsingham Railway, where it dwarfs the line's Garratt locomotive *Norfolk Hero*. *RJA*

REDISCOVERING RAILWAYS

TROWSE SWING BRIDGE: Class '33' No 33027, returning to its native Southern Region after an appearance at Crown Point Depot Open Day, meets Class '47' No 47587 with the 15.30 from Liverpool Street on the swing bridge at Trowse. By this time, September 1983, the bridge was in urgent need of replacement.

The extension of electrification to Norwich provided the opportunity to replace the bridge, with its 15mph speed restriction, and a new bridge was built a few yards upstream, coming into use in February 1987. Electric current is carried over the swinging section of the new single-line bridge by means of a fixed overhead bar, which connects with the catenary wires at each end of the bridge. The fixed overhead is clearly seen in this picture, as Class '86' electric loco No 86238 heads for Crown Point Depot. *Both D. C. Pearce*

NORWICH VICTORIA: In the immediate post-war years Victoria station was completely re-organised and claimed to possess the country's most up-to-date goods yards. Storage for about 500 wagons of coal and other merchandise was needed daily at Norwich rail depots and the new yard gave much needed relief to Thorpe. Victoria station had not been used as a passenger station since 1916, although it was used as a coal concentration depot until 1986.

The area has since suffered the same fate as so many former railway yards, namely a supermarket complex and a car park. The building to the left of the three-arch road bridge is, however, still clearly visible today. *Norfolk Railway Society Archive/DGS*

NORWICH DEPOT: The final steam locomotive to be allocated to Norwich Depot was fittingly an ex-GER design, 'J17' 0-6-0 No 65567. Framed in the sand hopper it potters around in Norwich shed yard on 25 March 1962, less than a week before being transferred away. Brush Type 2 No D5567 stands in front of the soon-to-be redundant coaling tower, whilst two BTH Type 1s of the D82XX series are also present.

The coaling tower was demolished soon afterwards and the area was taken over by Charringtons, the fuel distributors. In May 1991 the redundant hopper still stood in the fuel yard, with the loco shed building, although by now disused, still standing on the left.

By March 1998 the whole area was in the throes of a major redevelopment. The fuel tanks have gone, providing a clear view of a distant Class '158' running into the station, while on the left contractors are at work on the site of the old shed. *All RJA*

NORWICH THORPE: Brand new English Electric Type 4 No D205 waits to leave Norwich Thorpe station with a London express in 1958. At this time locomotives were still green with the British Railways roundel emblem and no yellow warning panel on the front, railwaymen wore old-style headgear, and schoolboys wore school caps and short trousers.

In 1998 the majority of London trains use platform 1, on the extreme left, while the other platforms are used by cross-country and local trains. On a fine May afternoon in 1998 the platforms are uncharacteristically deserted, enabling us to see how little the station has changed over the years. The only sign of activity is a Class '153' ticking over in the sidings on the right. Scaffolding encases the distinctive dome, as work continues on an extensive facelift of the station buildings. *Andrew Ingram/RJA*

NORFOLK

BUCKENHAM opened with the Yarmouth & Norwich Railway in 1844; 120 years later a Metro-Cammell DMU smokes away towards Norwich, passing a nicely contrasting pair of signals.

   Serving a scattered marshland community, it is remarkable that Buckenham station remains open today, although the 1998 weekday summer timetable shows that only one train a day is booked to call – and that only by request. The signals have gone, although the box survived until the late 1980s, and the station building is now in residential use. Class '86' electric loco No 86208 *City of Chester* is an unlikely visitor some 8 miles from the nearest catenary, bringing up the rear of a through train from Yarmouth to London. *A. E. Bennett/RJA*

YARMOUTH VAUXHALL: Having arrived from Norwich, 'D16/3' 4-4-0 No 62511 simmers at Yarmouth's Vauxhall terminus on a somewhat damp 31 August 1958. The unattended suitcase is a sign of more relaxed times – in the 1990s it would probably cause an evacuation of the entire area!

In July 1991 an elderly DMU set stands at the spot where No 62511 stood in 1958. Almost isolated in a sea of seemingly never-ending road traffic, Yarmouth's surviving railway station stands adjacent to the Asda superstore; very matter-of-fact with no frills, as befits today's railway, there is none the less a good-sized forecourt even including a bookstall with the old words 'W. H. Smith & Son' discernable under the new name. The platforms curve away to the left with signal box and semaphore starter signals at the platform end, rusty sidings to the right and just beyond the station the tracks with walkways intact which formed the extensive coach sidings of past years. The station canopy has been removed back to the buffer stops and forecourt. *A. E. Bennett/DGS*

YARMOUTH QUAYSIDE TRAMWAY: The tramway from Yarmouth Vauxhall to the quayside was for a few years the home of the 'Y10' 0-4-0 double-ended Sentinel locomotives, originally used on the Wisbech & Upwell line. With the crew keeping a sharp lookout, No 8186 makes its way along Hall Quay with a goods train from the docks. The 'NE' lettering dates this scene in the late '40s/early '50s.

Forty years on, the facades of the buildings on Hall Quay are largely unchanged, but motorists no longer need fear the passage of a lengthy goods train. The complicated one-way system is, however, perhaps an even greater hazard. *Dr I. C. Allen/RJA*

YARMOUTH SOUTH TOWN: Looking at the reduced railway scene of the 1990s, it is often difficult to recall just how much land even a medium-sized station could take up. This is well illustrated by this view of the approach to Yarmouth South Town, seen from a down 'B1'-hauled train in February 1959.

Once the terminus of London expresses, South Town declined in importance during the 1960s, and the surviving 'pay train' service to Lowestoft was withdrawn in 1970. Inevitably, the central site soon disappeared underneath new roads, superstores and industrial units, and the previous viewpoint can no longer be used. However, the buildings on the right appear in the earlier picture, and the distinctive town hall clock-tower remains on the skyline. *A. E. Bennett/RJA*

NORTH WALSHAM MAIN: Class '58' No 58045 stands at North Walsham with a tanker train for Parkeston Quay on 15 April 1997. The old station buildings are complete, although threatened with demolition.

On 4 March 1998 Class '47' No 47519 was on the same working, and witnessed the demolition of the final remnants of the down-side station buildings. The up side building has already gone.

Some two months later a new shelter, incorporating spandrels from the old station canopy, was being erected on the up platform. Class '37' No 37194 provides a further variety of motive power for the Parkeston Quay tanks on 1 May 1998. *All D. C. Pearce*

G. E. R.
——
From _____

TO

NORTH WALSHAM

CROMER HIGH: 'B1' 4-6-0 No 61051 pulls out of the original GER terminus at Cromer, before passenger services were concentrated on Cromer Beach station in 1954. Goods trains continued to use the yard until 1960, after which the site stood derelict for some years.

I climbed up a steep embankment to reach this site and walked between stacks of bricks towards the parapet of the old bridge. New houses are being built on the site, and there is easier access to the area from the Norwich road, this being not the most convenient site for a station, on an escarpment overlooking and about a mile from the town centre. Here the M&GN scored with their Beach station, in a more favourable position near the town. A few hundred yards to the south-east of this spot the Norfolk & Suffolk joint line ran under the GE on its way north-westwards to join the M&GN line at Runton West Junction. I am standing where the telegraph pole was in the earlier picture; had I stepped back I would have fallen into the road, the bridge having long since gone! *M&GN Circle, E. Tuddenham/DGS*

REDISCOVERING RAILWAYS

CENTRAL NORFOLK
Wells, Dereham and Thetford

COLTISHALL: With a load of concrete beams from Lenwade, train 7Z61 passes the remains of Coltishall station on the branch from Wroxham to County School on 4 June 1968. Brush Type 2 No D5563 double-heads its blue-painted sister No D5545, a combination required for braking rather than haulage capacity. Freight traffic over this route declined during the 'seventies, and the line closed to all traffic in 1982.

Eight years later, the railway from Wroxham to Aylsham reopened, albeit on 15-inch gauge track. Although a new platform and passing loop have been built beyond the original platform end, the old station building at Coltishall has changed but little. A Bure Valley Railway train is negotiating the spring points out of the loop as it heads towards Wroxham behind loco No 24. Formerly on the Fairbourne Railway, No 24 was regauged and moved to Norfolk in the early summer of 1991. *Both RJA*

BUXTON: A special passenger train pauses by the substantial station building at Buxton on 2 May 1981. This proved to be the very last passenger working over the branch.

A Bure Valley Railway train passes the well-maintained buildings on its way to Aylsham on 19 April 1998. For much of its length the narrow-gauge line is paralleled by the public footpath seen to the left of the train. *Both RJA*

REEPHAM: A DMU heads west from the station on 17 September 1977, forming a special 'Silver Jubilee' train to mark the 25th anniversary of the withdrawal of passenger services from the Wroxham to County School line. Organised by the Aylsham & District Rail Action Committee, the train ran as far as Lenwade, using the 1960 Themelthorpe curve.

The public footpath on the former railway line is clearly evident in this picture dating from 15 July 1997, while both the former station building and goods shed survive as reminders of earlier times. Nowadays the station building is a tea-room and bicycle hire centre catering for users of the Marriotts Way footpath, which joins the Bure Valley path at Aylsham and follows the GER route to Themelthorpe, before turning southwards along the former Midland & Great Northern Railway (M&GN) trackbed into Norwich. *Both D. C. Pearce*

THEMELTHORPE (1): Early in the BR era, a 'J17' 0-6-0 heads a lengthy cattle train along the GE line and under the girder bridge carrying the M&GN at Themelthorpe. The two railways also crossed at Fakenham but there the M&GN passed beneath the Great Eastern. The railwayman posing on the bridge could indicate that a special stop was made in the middle of the section to enable this picture to be taken. Could such an irregularity have taken place? Headquarters was certainly many miles away from this remote spot!

Standing in the stubble of a field on a hot late summer's day in 1990 looking at the remains of a railway bridge, it was hard to visualize that two railways crossed at this point. The embankment on either side of the bridge has been cut away to allow tractor access into the fields on each side of the cutting. A few hundred yards to the east is the trackbed of the Themelthorpe Curve, opened in 1960 to avoid a lengthy round trip of some 64 miles to points only a mile apart, Norwich's former City and Thorpe stations. *M&GN Circle, E. Tuddenham/DGS*

THEMELTHORPE (2): The driver and fireman look out for the photographer as 'E4' 2-4-0 No 62782 comes under the road bridge at Themelthorpe with the 11.15 train from Dereham to Norwich via Foulsham on 2 July 1949. This typical East Anglian branch-line train is formed of a quite remarkable selection of coaches from the LNER and its constituents.

In 1991 it was necessary to cross a short strand of barbed wire, walk across a few yards of muddy meadow and down a steep slope to reach the same spot. Much vegetation has sprung up during the ensuing years, but the bridge still bears the stone inscription 'G.E.R. 1918'. *M&GN Circle, E. Tuddenham/DGS*

FOULSHAM, the last station on the branch before the junction at County School, looking east back towards Aylsham. In the early years of this century the station saw nine trains a day, and the Second World War revived its fortunes, as with many other stations near RAF bases, but this activity was wound down during the 'fifties, the station closing in October 1964.

Foulsham station today is in private occupation, and the present owners were very cooperative, showing my wife and I photographs of the station in its heyday. They produce honey and the air is heavy with a sweet smell and the bustle of bees. *M&GN Circle, E. Tuddenham/DGS*

COUNTY SCHOOL: The headcode disc shows that 'D1' 4-4-0 No 3062, a GNR design introduced to the area by the LNER, is heading a train from the Wroxham branch as it pulls into the station at County School soon after the Second World War. Only the station dog provides any sign of life. The single lines from Wells and Wroxham converged at a point a mile or so north of County School, and ran independently, each with its own set of mileposts, to the station. Most trains ran through to Dereham or beyond, so the terminal and run-round facilities at the outer face of the island platform on the right of the picture were rarely used. Nevertheless, the station retained a rural junction atmosphere, if not its collection of enamel signs, right up to the withdrawal of passenger trains in October 1964.

Goods trains continued to run through the increasingly neglected station for many years, but by the mid-1980s the traffic had gone and the tracks had been torn up. However, a preservation group then moved in and made considerable progress in restoring the site. Visiting steam locomotive *Sir Berkeley* darkens the sky, while two Class '20' diesels occupy the other platforms on 18 July 1993.

Sadly the group was forced to quit as a result of financial problems, and in the spring of 1998 the weeds were beginning to take a hold once more. *D. Thompson/RJA (2)*

RYBURGH: Unlike the other lines to the North Norfolk coast, the Wells line was not swamped with heavy weekend excursion traffic. Those specials which did run were often for the benefit of pilgrims visiting the shrines at Walsingham, and one such train travels through typical mid-Norfolk countryside just south of Ryburgh station on 16 August 1959, with 'D16/3' 4-4-0 No 62544 at the head of nine corridor coaches. On the far horizon is the water tower on the Sennowe Park estate.

To find this spot today one must take an obscure unclassified road which runs roughly parallel and to the west of the A1067, and beneath a road bridge one finds the usual signs of a defunct railway, post-and-wire fencing and linear scrub, although, of course, this line was closed only comparatively recently. The water tower in the previous picture is just visible again on the horizon. *M&GN Circle, E. Tuddenham/DGS*

FAKENHAM EAST: The station at Fakenham remained substantially intact following the withdrawal of passenger trains in 1964, although inevitably there was some rationalisation of the trackwork. This was the scene on 21 April 1979 when the station played host to the 'Fakenham Flyer', a privately chartered special train composed of two Cravens two-car DMUs.

The 'Fakenham Flyer' proved to be the last passenger train to visit the town, as the station was closed completely early in the following year. The railway land was far too valuable to stay derelict for long, and when this picture was taken in 1988 the station site had vanished under a housing development, although one crossing gate and the goods platform remained. Since then further building has removed even these reminders of the railway. *RJA/DGS*

WIGHTON was an undistinguished halt about half a mile from the village. The station was and is approached by a track from the Fakenham–Wells road, and is probably as basic a station as you can get; passengers alighting here had to travel in a specified coach because of the limited platform length. It is seen here on closure day, 3 October 1964.

I sat on an overgrown embankment in the late summer of 1990 to get this picture of the narrow gauge train on its way from Walsingham to Wells. The new railway runs a distance of approximately 5 miles and claims to be the longest 10¼-inch narrow gauge railway in the country. *RJA/DGS*

WELLS-NEXT-THE-SEA boasted a compact little terminus with its freight facilities rubbing shoulders with the loco servicing area. The van on the extreme left peers from the goods shed, which was also the loco shed building, whilst the proximity of the cattle pens to the turntable and water tower makes one wonder how the beasts reacted to the sounds of steam engines being serviced! A 'D16/3' 4-4-0 waits by the turntable in August 1956.

Today we have yet another industrial estate, the fate which has befallen so many redundant station sites! Part of the mill building survives, but is now an antiques centre. A good clue here is the road name 'Great Eastern Way'.
W. J. Naunton/DGS

STANHOE: Waiting for the train at Stanhoe on the Wells to Heacham line shortly before closure in June 1952. The smart young man, station cat, rudimentary shelter and oil lamps are all worthy of note, as the track curves away into the distance across the open North Norfolk countryside. Unusually, Stanhoe station had no sidings and was therefore a 'passenger only' station; however, the occasional goods train continued to pass through on its way to Burnham Market until 1964.

After the line closed, Stanhoe station was converted into a private house. Although the shelter has gone, the station building and wooden hut are little changed externally. The dip two-thirds of the way along the platform has become a bit more pronounced, and the whole site has a considerably more sylvan air about it. *D. Thompson/DGS*

NORTH ELMHAM: Returning to County School, the first and only station on the line south towards Dereham was North Elmham, where traffic to the granary kept the line open throughout the 1980s. On 26 April 1984 a special train chartered by William McAlpine visited the line as part of a three-day tour of East Anglian railways, and at North Elmham Class '31' No 31222 needed to shunt the grain wagons out of the way before it could run round its coaches. In the foreground is the brick base of the signal box.

It is a very different scene on 24 March 1998, as the granary has been demolished and replaced by housing. Some rusty, overgrown tracks remain in place, and may one day be used again, as restoration of train services north of Dereham is a long-term aim of the Mid Norfolk Railway. *Both RJA*

DEREHAM (1): With the Norwich to Wells line going north, and the Kings Lynn line running west, Dereham was a busy country junction in its time. As the lines converged facing the Wells direction, passenger trains between Norwich and Kings Lynn had to reverse in the station, although there was an avoiding line used by freight and excursion traffic not needing to call at Dereham. The complex was controlled by no fewer than four signal boxes, Dereham North, South, West and, rather spoiling the geographical completeness, Central. It is the imposing Central box which dominates the scene as Brush Type 2 No D5661 shunts the daily Fakenham goods in the busy yard on 30 May 1969. Although by now passenger services to both north and west had been withdrawn, the passenger trains to Norwich would continue to run for another four months, whilst regular freight traffic was to continue until the end of the 1980s.

Following the closure of the Wells line to passenger trains in 1964, the freight service was cut back first to Fakenham, then progressively to Ryburgh and North Elmham as traffic declined. Latterly little used, the line from Wymondham to Dereham itself closed in 1989, and by the summer of 1991 the remaining tracks at Dereham were in a state of limbo, awaiting an uncertain future.

After a lot of hard work, the Mid Norfolk Railway began to run trains southwards out of Dereham station as far as Yaxham in July 1997, and they have high hopes of extending the service over the whole 11 miles to Wymondham. A further boost during 1988 was the use of the line to transport military vehicles to and from Robertson Barracks, near Dereham. Although a road cuts across the former railway land in the foreground, a Class '20' loco and DMU stock provide positive signs for the future. *RJA/DGS/RJA*

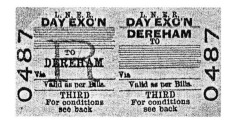

DEREHAM (2): No, these pictures are not in the wrong order! Dereham station looked extremely woebegone in June 1994, shortly after the tracks through the platforms had been lifted.

Just four years later, on 10 May 1998, the scene has been transformed, with rolling-stock occupying the relaid track, and a single-unit railcar, No M55006, waiting to leave for Yaxham. *DGS/RJA*

DEREHAM (3): With Dereham West signal box in the background, a Class 'E4' 2-4-0 approaches the station with a train from the Kings Lynn direction, probably in the early 1950s.

This approach to Dereham has altered out of all recognition, with a road cutting across what is otherwise derelict land. However, the buffer stop on the left has managed to survive all the changes. *South Devon Railway Museum/DGS*

WENDLING: Taking the Kings Lynn line from Dereham, the first station served the village of Wendling, and is seen here slumbering in the morning sunshine in July 1964. A westbound train is signalled, and a solitary prospective passenger paces the platform.

Turn to the north off the old A47 trunk road some 4 miles west of Dereham along an unclassified road which passes over the Dereham bypass, then look towards Swaffham and you are looking down on the site of Wendling station. To the left, at right angles to the bypass, there are some bungalows; the one visible here is in the same row as the one in the earlier picture, which looks to be of an earlier design (the old goods shed masks the site of this newer bungalow). *D. Thompson/DGS*

SWAFFHAM: Until 1964 Swaffham was the junction for the branch line to Thetford. The destination blind shows that the DMU, waiting, perhaps optimistically, for custom on 30 March 1959, is bound for the branch. Passenger services on the Dereham to Kings Lynn section outlasted those on the branch by only four years, and Swaffham station closed completely in September 1968.

Twenty-two years later the station building appears substantially intact, and there is evidence of renovation and extension to the original structure. The yard, like so many others in small East Anglian towns, has become enveloped

HOLME HALE: 'One and a half to Swaffham, please.' The porter shepherds his two customers and their pram towards the morning train from Thetford as it pulls into Holme Hale station on 17 September 1962. Both the friendliness of the rural branch line and the reason for its latter-day unprofitablility are shown in this scene.

Holme Hale is still a well-kept station with signal cabin intact. On the north side, the old goods shed has been converted into an attractive dwelling house, while alongside is a well preserved goods van painted in bauxite and sporting the initials LMS (not its original lettering). A weathervane with a locomotive design completes the scene.

WATTON: The Thetford & Watton Railway was opened in 1869 and the whole route from Thetford to Swaffham was taken over by the Great Eastern Railway 11 years later, to become another typical GER branch line. Watton was the principal town served by the line, but even here the arrival of the afternoon train on the final day produces only a solitary onlooker. The platforms here were staggered, and the train is passing the down platform before coming to a stand at the up.

Following closure the station site was totally redeveloped, and an Ordnance Survey map proved useful to find it, a quarter of a mile out of town on the Norwich road. The platform area is part of a Council depot, while the yard has disappeared under an industrial estate. A plaque on the wall of the building on the right reminds passers-by that this was the site of a railway station, while the imposing former Railway Hotel looks out on a much changed scene. *Both RJA*

WRETHAM & HOCKHAM was the last station on the line before Thetford. The platform is showing signs of neglect as a 'last day' train pulls away on 13 June 1964.

Visited in October 1990, the station is in private occupation. The owner has put in a lot of work here and the station buildings are in excellent shape, having formerly been owned by the last station master. I was told that the platform was beyond repair and had to be demolished, although the lip remains. The original small lamp hut survives and is seen along the platform at the rear, while the trackbed across the road is now a private garden with a lawn and conifer trees, providing nothing to indicate that a railway ever ran here. *RJA/DGS*

REDISCOVERING RAILWAYS

THETFORD: The plain unrelieved blue livery of the 1970s is now thankfully only a memory, although no doubt some will recall it with affection! During that period, a down train leaves Thetford for Norwich, formed of a mixture of Metro-Cammell, Cravens and Gloucester RC&W diesel multiple unit vehicles.

The line through Thetford had been opened during the 1840s as part of the first through route from London to Norwich, but by the mid-1970s was used largely by stopping local services, with the occasional through trains to the Midlands or North. The line south to Bury, the southern section of the Thetford & Watton Railway, lost its passenger service in 1953, but retained a goods service until 1960. From the late 1980s onwards, however, the cross-country services were much improved with the use of 'Sprinters', and the current timetable provided a virtually hourly service throughout the day between Norwich and Peterborough and beyond. One such train, formed of a Class '158' 'Express' unit, leaves Thetford for Norwich, as a Metro-Cammell DMU enters with a Cambridge train. *D. C. Pearce/DGS*

WYMONDHAM: South of Dereham was this country junction, where the lines to Dereham and Forncett left the Thetford–Norwich route. A typical local train of the 1950s pauses on the last lap of its journey to Norwich, with 'D16/3' 4-4-0 No 62522 at the head.

Wymondham station became unstaffed in the mid-1960s and the flint-built building fell into a state of disrepair. It has now been restored and is used as a piano showroom and period tea-room. In essence the scene has changed little over the years, as a Class '56' No 56065 heads towards Norwich with a Redland stone train. *W. J. Naunton/DGS*

THE MIDLAND & GREAT NORTHERN

Cromer to South Lynn

GORLESTON-ON-SEA: A joint venture between the M&GN and the GER, the Norfolk & Suffolk Joint Railway from Yarmouth to Lowestoft did not open until 1903. Traffic never matched the ambitions of the builders, and the comprehensive station facilities were rarely taxed. A Derby lightweight DMU set heading a Metro-Cammell unit appears lost within Gorleston-on-Sea station in the late 1950s.

After a life of only 67 years the line was closed entirely, and in 1991 the site of the station was being incorporated in a new road scheme. Only the distant road bridge survived as a reminder of the railway.

In May 1998 the road scheme was complete. Only the buildings to the immediate right of the bridge provide a link with the earlier pictures. *M&GN Circle, E. Tuddenham/ RJA (2)*

HOPTON-ON-SEA. The Norfolk & Suffolk Joint Committee believed in lavish station facilities, but in most cases the traffic never really materialised. Only a handful of passengers will patronise this Derby lightweight DMU which is arriving at Hopton-on-Sea on a Yarmouth to Lowestoft working in September 1962. At this time the line was enjoying a brief final flourish, handling all the East Suffolk line Yarmouth traffic following the closure of the direct line from Beccles three years earlier.

This is not an easy site to find nowadays, a housing estate having been built across the track. The station master's house still stands, with a visible clue near the door, and a friendly (railway enthusiast) policeman pointed out the old gates to the goods yard to the right of the station master's house; but it is none the less almost impossible to envisage yesteryear's scene. *M&GN Circle, E. Tuddenham/DGS*

YARMOUTH BEACH: The 1923 Grouping scarcely affected the M&GN, which remained an independent concern until 1936. Following the LNER takeover, many of the former M&GN locos lingered on for a few years before being replaced; here, renumbered in the duplicate list and bearing the initials of its new owners, 0-6-0T No 016 shunts at Yarmouth Beach on 14 March 1939. Beyond is another sign of the LNER influence, ex-GNR 'C12' 4-4-2T No 4015, which had been imported to handle trains to Lowestoft. No 016 was to survive another ten years, coming into British Railways ownership before being withdrawn in August 1949. The 'Joint' outlasted the loco by less than a decade, and by August 1959 Yarmouth Beach station was trackless and desolate.

Since then the station area has been a coach and car park, utilising the original station buildings and offices until the late 1980s. Unfortunately my recent visit coincided with a heavy summer shower, and looking across where the goods yards once stood, only the houses in the background are identifiable. Passing holidaymakers probably thought that I was mad taking a photograph of a car park in the pouring rain! *H.C. Casserley/DGS*

POTTER HEIGHAM: The GNR somersault signal has dropped to allow a Class '4MT' 2-6-0 to run into Potter Heigham station from the east, while in the distance a sister loco waits for the line to clear before it can continue its journey. In this scene from the late 1950s, the ancient buses on the left merit more than a passing glance.

Much of the M&GN trackbed hereabouts has been incorporated in improvements to the A149 road, and in 1998 the windpump surveys an altogether less interesting scene. The original fencing can be traced in the hedgerow to the left, but there is no trace of the railway in this picture. However, the curve of the road clearly follows that of the track in the previous view. *Dr I. C. Allen/RJA*

REDISCOVERING RAILWAYS

STALHAM: In addition to trains to Melton Constable and points further west, certain 'short' workings operated from Yarmouth Beach, terminating at intermediate stations such as Potter Heigham and Aylsham. One such train was the Wednesdays and Saturdays only 12 noon from Yarmouth to Stalham, which is seen here awaiting its 1.05 pm return to Yarmouth at the well-kept station on 27 August 1958. The four Gresley coaches are headed by Ivatt 'Mogul' No 43157.

Tucked away in a corner at the junction of the busy A149 and the B1151 to Sea Palling, Stalham station has in its retirement become a Council depot with the usual debris which accumulates in such places. Much of the goods yard and trackbed is a car park with an extension for overflow during the summer season, although it was nowhere near full when we visited it. The road bridge has been swept away in the new road development. *M&GN Circle, E. Tuddenham/DGS*

MUNDESLEY-ON-SEA station was a latecomer to the railway map, the branch from North Walsham having only been opened as late as 1898. On 15 May 1960 'J15' 0-6-0 No 65469 stands in the station, the loco and branch having been hired by enthusiasts of the Norfolk Railway Society for a day's driving and firing instruction; the amateur enginemen certainly appear to be producing a good head of steam! One of several camping coaches based at Mundesley in the latter years stands in the bay platform, while a couple of coal wagons occupy the goods yard.

Traffic on the line never justified the station's three through platforms and a bay, and the service from North Walsham was withdrawn in October 1964, a victim of the Beeching Report; goods traffic finished later in the year. In the present-day picture a lady cleans her car on a housing estate on the outskirts of Mundesley, probably unaware that the railway once occupied the land. Only the roof of the distant white-painted building in the 1960 picture provides a common element in the two views. *W. J. Naunton/RJA*

OVERSTRAND: The Norfolk & Suffolk Joint line from Mundesley to Cromer had a life of only some 47 years, closing completely in April 1953. On the last day of services, ex-GER 'F6' 2-4-2T No 67228 and two GER coaches forming the 12.05 from Cromer leave Overstrand station.

Not too easy to find today, a couple of miles out of Cromer on the B1159 opposite a small garage a stony private road leads up to the station. This is now private land but a footpath passes near the east side of the old station. The subway under the trackbed is still intact, but even more extraordinary is the covered walkway from the platform to the subway which is also still in existence. *M&GN Circle, E. Tuddenham/DGS*

CROMER BEACH: On a raw October day in 1968, Brush Type 2 No D5665 waits in Cromer yard with coal empties for Norwich. The overall roof of the passenger station provides a degree of shelter from the driving rain.

Class '153' No 153311 waits to leave Cromer on a Norwich service on 21 April 1998. A supermarket has been built on the former goods yard, the overall roof has gone and the line has been truncated. Scaffolding surrounds the station building, which, after being threatened with demolition for some years, was restored, converted into licensed premises and opened as Buffers Bar in June 1998. *Both RJA*

RUNTON WEST JUNCTION: The signalman at Runton West Junction near Cromer prepares to hand over the tablet for the single-line section on to Sheringham. Cromer Beach, the former M&GN station in the resort, is a terminus, and trains from Norwich to Sheringham have to reverse there, although at one time an avoiding line ran from Runton West Junction to Newstead Lane Junction, forming a triangle. The Brush Type 2 in the picture has no doubt run round its train at Cromer Beach before continuing its journey. To the right the tracks of the avoiding line to Newstead Lane Junction appear dull and unused, thus dating the picture at around 1960/1, the spur having closed in the former year.

On 1 June 1991, a Class '158' unit passes the site of Runton West Junction box. The brand new 'Sprinter' is filling in time on local workings before going into service on the cross-country routes from Norwich to the Midlands and the North. To train crews and passengers alike, the contrast with the 30-year-old Metro-Cammell trains normally used on the Sheringham line was no doubt noticeable! The route of the avoiding line has vanished beneath the trees, but the depression in the cutting side to the left of the picture indicates where the signal box once stood. *M&GN Circle, E. Tuddenham/ RJA*

SHERINGHAM: The station at Sheringham was shared by the GER and the M&GN from 1906 onwards. A DMU, possibly working on the Norwich Thorpe–Sheringham–Melton Constable–Norwich City circuit, stands at the platform on 28 February 1959.

REDISCOVERING RAILWAYS

From 1964 onwards Sheringham became the terminus of a single-line branch from Cromer, and as the station facilities were far too large for this remaining service a basic single-line platform was built a little nearer Cromer. The redundant facilities were taken over by preservationists, and the station is now the headquarters of the North Norfolk Railway. On the left-hand platform, the original buildings and canopy survive, while from the right-hand platform a small boy admires the railway's former 'Brighton Belle' Pullman car. *A.E. Bennett/RJA*

NORFOLK

WEYBOURNE: The closure of the M&GN as a through route deprived the still substantial freight traffic from Norwich City of a direct route to the Midlands and beyond. Goods trains from Norwich had therefore to travel some 60 miles via Melton Constable and Cromer before getting back to Norwich Thorpe and its links with the rest of the country (see Themelthorpe, pages 38-39). With the North Sea in the background, 'WD' 2-8-0 No 90559, a remarkably clean member of the class, heads one such train down the bank towards Weybourne on a summer's day in 1959.

The section of line from Weybourne to Holt was lifted after closure in 1964, and was subsequently relaid by the North Norfolk Railway. The concrete hut has survived all the changes, while beyond the railway the traditional field pattern is substantially unchanged as railbus No E79963 heads for Holt. *M&GN Circle, E. Tuddenham/RJA*

HOLT: The M&GN's Cromer line survived the otherwise wholesale 1959 closure and passenger trains continued to run to Melton Constable from Sheringham until April 1964. On the final afternoon of services, two Metro-Cammell DMUs pass at Holt station, the last daylight use of the loop there. *RJA*

Freight lingered on to the end of 1964, and the track was then lifted. During the '70s the derelict station languished before the bypass was built. The preserved North Norfolk Railway had hopes of extending their line to the old station but the realignment of the road and removal of a dangerous rail bridge put paid to these hopes. However, a good compromise has been reached with a new station on the north side of the road, a short distance from the town. *D.C. Pearce*

The old station in October 1988, and all has been swept away, although a good clue is still in sight – the mill on the right remains, looking down on a very different scene. *DGS*

NORFOLK

CORPUSTY: On the line between North Walsham and Melton Constable, Corpusty was a typical country station. Seen here from the roadbridge, a short goods yard and some cattle pens are visible. At least Corpusty station was in the village, which could not be said of too many stations on the M&GN – a traveller once enquired at a local pub why a certain station was so far from the village, and was told 'because it's near the railway'. From Corpusty the line was doubled for some 18 miles to Raynham Park.

The same view in October 1988, and the whole area is under grass. It is now a sports centre with sleeping accommodation provided at the station house. A lone stroller exercises his dog. *Ray Meek Collection/DGS*

DRAYTON: After the closure of the majority of the M&GN system, the Norwich branch continued to carry quite considerable freight traffic. Even after Norwich City station itself closed, the line continued in use for the conveyance of concrete products from Lenwade and sand from Drayton. Brush Type 2 No D5579 shunts the sand train in Drayton yard on 14 April 1969, with the traditional goods sheds and loading dock well in evidence. This traffic survived a year or two longer, but by 1973 the tracklifting gang was at work here.

Today the area is occupied by a small industrial estate, although the houses in the background are easily identifiable. With a little hindsight, how useful a light railway would be now with the vast Thorpe Marriott estate just half a mile away, which makes a busy road even busier. *RJA/DGS*

LENWADE (1) was the next but one station along the line towards Melton Constable. Brush Type 2 No D5545 waits at the station with a Norwich City to Norwich Thorpe goods working on 4 June 1968.

Nearly 30 years later, the Marriotts Way footpath follows the trackbed through the station. There are detail differences to the boarded-up station building, but despite the loss of the signal box, the rails and one crossing gate, the scene is remarkably similar. *Both RJA*

LENWADE (2): After closure to passengers, occasional railtours provided the opportunity for enthusiasts to travel over the line to Lenwade. Class '31' No 31160 heads one such train just south of the station on 3 October 1976. The concrete milepost, a distinctive feature of the M&GN, indicates the distance from South Lynn.

Some 15 years after the track has been lifted, milepost 42½ still provides a link with the past in March 1998. *Both RJA*

WHITWELL & REEPHAM: Trains to and from Norwich City pass at an otherwise deserted Whitwell & Reepham station on the final day of passenger services on the line, 28 February 1959.

Surrounded by considerable tree growth, the platforms, station building and fencing remain in March 1998, while the foundations of the waiting shelter can clearly be made out on the far platform. Much of the Norwich branch has been incorporated in the long-distance Marriotts Way footpath, which makes its way between the platforms here. *A. E. Bennett/RJA*

MELTON CONSTABLE (1): The activity at Melton West Junction belies the fact that this picture was taken on the very last day of the M&GN as a through route. A '4MT' 2-6-0 pulls away from the station stop with the final through train from Yarmouth Beach to Leicester and Birmingham, as a down freight arrives with another '4MT' at the head. The Cromer line curves away to the right, above the ex-GER restaurant car which provided refreshments on the 'Leicester'.

An incredible difference in today's viewpoint! The fields are under cultivation and the line of electric poles almost bisects the angle of the old lines to Holt and Fakenham. However, the tower known as Belle Vue is just visible in the left background of both pictures – originally a smock mill, it is alleged to have a fine view of Norwich and the sea.
A.E. Bennett/DGS

MELTON CONSTABLE (2): Another of the versatile Ivatt 'Moguls', South Lynn's No 43107, stands at Melton Constable with a Peterborough to Yarmouth train alongside a splendid signal post controlling the goods line.

Yesteryear's 'Crewe of North Norfolk' is today an industrial estate. Using the house on the right as a marker, I stood (with permission) in the spring of 1991 among a line of small conifers just about where the platform ended; where the '4MT' once stood a car was parked beside a brick-built club house. *Doug Watts/DGS*

THURSFORD: Ivatt 'Mogul' No 43154 passes a typical M&GN signal box and crossing gates as it runs into the country station at Thursford in 1958. *M&GN Circle, E. Tuddenham*

The second picture of the sequence shows the derelict station in the mid-'sixties. *DGS*

'Where exactly did the signal box stand?' I asked the elderly gentleman exercising his dog. 'Right here,' and he indicated a spot some 20 yards in front of where I was standing. The old goods shed is now used as a Council depot, and the house in the 1958 picture is just visible beyond the trees. *DGS*

FAKENHAM WEST: Despite early dieselisation elsewhere in the area, the M&GN, except for the Norwich and Cromer branches, remained very much a steam railway to the end. During the final years, however, two of the Norwich branch services were extended through to Fakenham West, thus providing a rare diesel railcar turn on the main line. This Metro-Cammell unit has just crossed from the up to the down platform at Fakenham, and is about to return to Melton Constable.

The trackbed now leads to the Gallows Sports Centre and Caravan Park, and a builders merchant's yards cover the whole area. However, a small length of platform remains, under the lip of which a plate reminds us that the Lynn & Fakenham Railway reached here in 1876; this momento was very much the initiative of the late Peter Fitzjohn. The concrete base of the footbridge steps remain on the old platform. *Doug Watts/DGS*

In the spring of 1965, whilst I was taking photographs at Fakenham West station, a trio of workmen arrived and promptly set about the signal box, which was positioned just across the road. I was advised to hurry up or there wouldn't be much left – a case of being in the right place at the right time! *DGS*

RAYNHAM PARK: A feature of the M&GN was the Whitaker tablet exchange apparatus which enabled single-line tablets to be exchanged at speed, thus obviating a potential source of delay on the long single-line sections. The apparatus is ready for use beside the cab as '4F' 0-6-0 No 43954 passes through Raynham Park before running on to the single-line section to East Rudham. The '4Fs' were regular visitors to the M&GN, particularly on summer Saturdays, and this Nottingham-based loco is heading homewards with the 8.19 am train from Yarmouth Beach to Chesterfield on 2 August 1958.

On 13 July 1991 the summer meeting of the M&GN Circle was held at Raynham Park station and the opportunity was taken to match the old photograph taken from the signal box steps. The station master's house on the other side of the trackbed is clearly visible, the station building and signal box are in private occupation and in excellent repair, and a good effort has been made to preserve the old railway atmosphere in a sylvan setting. *M&GN Circle, E. Tuddenham/DGS*

EAST RUDHAM: Seen again from the signal box, Class '4MT' No 43110 stands at East Rudham station with a lengthy up cattle special on 21 May 1958. These Ivatt-designed locos replaced a miscellaneous selection of ageing motive power on the M&GN section from the early 1950s, and proved very successful on all types of traffic. Those allocated to the M&GN were fitted with the tablet exchange apparatus for use on single-line sections, and this can be seen fixed to the side of the tender of 43110.

Following the closure of the majority of the M&GN to passenger traffic on 28 February 1959, East Rudham became the terminus of a freight line from Kings Lynn, and for a few years generated a worthwhile grain traffic. Final closure came in 1968, and today the yard and trackbed are in commercial use. The goods shed in the background is still standing, while the station buildings, although empty, were in a good state of repair and had changed but little over the years. *M&GN Circle, E. Tuddenham/RJA*

GAYTON ROAD: On a bright winter morning in the late 1950s, Ivatt '4MT' No 43158 sweeps through Gayton Road station in fine style with the Yarmouth Beach to Birmingham express, an old GER buffet car rattling along at the front of the train. The tall Great Northern somersault signal with its repeater arm was a distinctive feature of the station, and the goods yard was still serving its scattered rural community.

With the passage of time a young wood has enveloped the site of the station, and only the platform end emerges from the greenery. The whole area is being landscaped, and the elevated 1959 viewpoint has been bulldozed away; on the right, however, the white shed with the sliding door has resisted change. *M&GN Circle, E. Tuddenham/RJA*

REDISCOVERING RAILWAYS

SOUTH LYNN: With its loco shed and marshalling yards, South Lynn was an important traffic centre on the M&GN. There was also a physical connection with the GER lines into that company's Kings Lynn station, over which a regular push-pull service operated. In the late 1950s Class 'C12' 4-4-2T No 67386 passes some early examples of colour light signals as it leaves South Lynn with this shuttle service at the start of its 5-minute journey to the former GER station.

The station at South Lynn was demolished soon after the 1959 closure, and the Kings Lynn bypass now cuts diagonally across the site. Some of the tracks survived until the 1990s to serve the sugar-beet factory, and the sleeper indentations in the foreground of this April 1998 view testify to fairly recent lifting. The gateposts on the left provide the only link with the earlier picture; although the exhaust of the 'C12' obscures the right-hand one, the other can be made out above the top right-hand corner of the black hut. *Dr I. C. Allen/RJA*

GAZETTEER OF NORFOLK'S RAILWAYS

Compiled by Geoffrey Body

Norfolk has surviving railway lines radiating from Norwich to Sheringham, Yarmouth, Lowestoft, Ipswich and Ely, and also the line south from Kings Lynn. Standard gauge preservation activity is represented by the North Norfolk Railway line from Sheringham and the Mid-Norfolk Railway's County School-Wymondham scheme and is included in the Bressingham Steam Museum, near Diss.

There are narrow gauge operations over former BR trackbeds from Aylsham to Wroxham (Bure Valley Railway) and Walsingham to Wells (Wells & Walsingham Light Railway) and another scheme at Wells Harbour. The Marriott Way walk utilises the former Aylsham-Themelthorpe (GE) and Themelthorpe-Norwich (M&GN) trackbed, and the Cromer to Yarmouth Weavers' Way uses the old M&GN route from Aylsham to Stalham.

Great Eastern Railway

The Great Eastern Railway came into being on 7 August 1862 by the amalgamation of the Eastern Counties, Norfolk, East Anglian, Eastern Union and East Suffolk undertakings. The system covered the whole of East Anglia and grew to a total of 1,316 miles, which produced modest dividends of 2-3% prior to the Grouping of 1923, when it became a constituent of the London & North Eastern Railway.

Dereham-Wells

Stations: North Elmham (4.5m), County School (6m), Ryburgh (9.5m), Fakenham East (12m), Walsingham (17m).

Opening and closure: Dereham to Fakenham opened by the Norfolk Railway 20.3.1849, Fakenham to Wells by the Wells & Fakenham Railway 1.12.1857. Closed to passengers 5.10.1964 and to freight starting 31.10.1964.

Route and traffic: This was an easily graded 21.5-mile route through rural Norfolk carrying Norwich-Wells and Dereham-Aylsham-Norwich passenger services. Single track with passing loops at County School and Fakenham, the line had junctions at County School for the Aylsham line and at the Wells terminus for Heacham and the harbour branch. Freight included coal, grain and milk at North Elmham and shipment traffic from and to Wells harbour. The line also carried pilgrims to the Catholic shrine at Walsingham and bagged shellfish from Wells. Milk and bulk grain kept the southern section open after general closure and long enough for preservation activity to begin. Wells had a small loco depot and Wighton Halt lay on the section south to Walsingham, now used by narrow gauge trains of the Wells & Walsingham Light Railway.

Forncett-Wymondham

Station: Ashwellthorpe (3m)

Opening and closure: Opened by the GER to relieve Norwich area congestion 2.5.1881. Closed to passengers 10.9.1939 and to freight 4.8.1951.

Route and traffic: This 6.75-mile double-track route had a passenger service of six/seven trains each way daily, most with a London connection of sorts at Forncett. At various times through services from the Dereham line ran this way, together with Peterborough mail and Whitemoor freight services. However, use was never very heavy except in the war periods. After closure a portion of embankment track from the junction east of Wymondham was retained for stock storage until 1976.

Heacham-Wells

Stations: Sedgeford (2.75m), Docking (6.25m), Stanhoe (8.25m), Burnham Market (11.75m), Holkham (16m).

Opening and closure: Opened by the West Norfolk Junction Railway 17.8.1866. Passenger services ended 2.6.1952 and line severed by 1953 floods. Heacham-Burnham operated for freight as a light railway until 28.12.1964.

Route and traffic: This meandering single line with passing loops ran for 18.25 miles through the quiet fields of North Norfolk to pass north of Holkham Hall and into Wells. Train services reflected the rural patronage, but the line had definite character – the electric telegraph came to life unaided on windy days! One-engine-in-steam working applied over the 11.75-mile, 25mph freight spur prior to the 1964 closure.

Kings Lynn

Operating over an electrified route south from a simplified terminus, today's West Anglia Great Northern trains carry on a railway tradition first established by the Lynn & Ely Railway in 1846. In its heyday the rebuilt (1871) five-platform Kings Lynn terminus originated services to Liverpool Street, Norwich, March and Hunstanton together with a shuttle service round to South Lynn for the Spalding/Peterborough and Norwich/Cromer/Yarmouth services on the M&GN system. Kings Lynn had the full range of goods, granary, loco and livestock facilities as well as the 1846-48 Harbour and 1870 Docks branches. South Lynn had its own loco shed and a BSC factory.

Kings Lynn-Ely

Stations: Magdalen Road (6m), Stow Bardolph (8.5m), Downham Market (10.75m), Hilgay (15.5m), Littleport (21m).

Opening and closure: Opened by the Lynn & Ely Railway to Downham Market 27.10.1846, to Denver Road Gate January 1847 and to Ely 26.10.1847, by which time the L&E was part of the East Anglian Railway. Hilgay and Stow Bardolph closed to passengers 4.11.1963 and to goods 13.7.1964. Magdalen Road (now Watlington) closed 9.9.1968 and re-opened 5.5.1975.

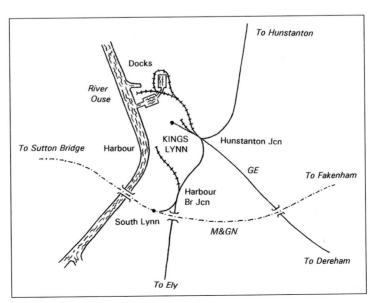

Route and traffic: This straight, flat, double-track Fenland route follows the River Ouse south from Kings Lynn and involves major viaduct crossings of that waterway and its Wissey tributary. Kings Lynn junctions with the Docks, Hunstanton and Harbour branches and with South Lynn were followed by those at Magdalen Road for Wisbech, and Denver for Stoke Ferry. In addition to its main-line business, the route used to carry Kings Lynn-March and Downham-Stoke Ferry trains. It handled extensive holidaymaker traffic to and from Hunstanton on summer Saturdays while freight was mainly inwards coal and outwards agricultural produce.

To the GER/LNER this was always a main line with Restaurant Car trains to Liverpool Street taking 160 minutes in the 1920s compared with 102 minutes to Kings Cross by today's West Anglia Great Northern electric trains.

Kings Lynn-Hunstanton

Stations: North Wootton (3.25m), Wolferton (6.25m), Dersingham (8.25m), Snettisham (10m), Heacham (13.25m).
Opening and closure: Opened by the Lynn & Hunstanton Railway 3.10.1862. Closed to goods 28.12.1964 and completely 5.5.1969.
Route and traffic: This 15.25-mile line along the flat heathland backing the eastern shoreline of The Wash was double to Wolferton then single with passing loops on to the substantial terminus at Hunstanton. Convenient for town and beach, this had four platform faces, excursion and goods sidings and a loco shed with turntable. The main business of the branch was holiday traffic for which it had through services from London and the Midlands, but it was also important as the Royal route to Sandringham via Wolferton station where the royal waiting room was preserved as a museum. Pre-closure economies included singling throughout in 1967.

Norwich

Thorpe station dates from 1886 when it replaced the original station of the Yarmouth & Norwich Railway opened on 30.4.1844 on a site that later became the goods depot. The eventual GER/LNER complex beside the River Wensum included the six-platform terminus with offices below the dramatic 76-foot central dome, a large adjacent goods depot with the loco depot beyond, then Wensum and Crown Point yard and sidings. Along the Ipswich route lay Trowse station, once noted for its livestock traffic, the connection to Victoria – the 1849-1916 Eastern

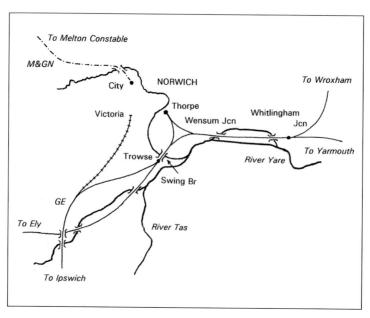

Union Railway terminus that later became a coal depot – and scrap and cattle market sidings. The M&GN's City station lay on the north side of the city. Anglia Railways electric trains now run to Liverpool Street, Central Trains to Peterborough and AR services to the coast.

Norwich-Brandon (Ely)

Stations: Trowse (1m), Hethersett (6.25m), Wymondham (10.25m), Spooner Row (12.75m), Attleborough (16m), Eccles Road (19.75m), Harling Road (22.75m), Thetford (30.5m), Brandon (37.75m).

Opening and closure: Norwich & Brandon Railway opened Brandon-Trowse 30.7.1845 and into Norwich proper 15.12.1845. Trowse closed to passengers 5.9.1939 and Hethersett 31.1.1966.

Route and traffic: Completion of the swing bridge over the Wensum at Norwich and of the connection with the Eastern Counties Railway at Brandon gave Norwich its first rail link to London in 1845. The double-track route then maintained this main-line status for over 100 years, carrying a local service to Ely and through expresses for Liverpool Street, Peterborough and the GN&GE Joint line. Freight services from Whitemoor also made extensive use of the route, while local traffic included cider from Attleborough and pit-props from Brandon. Today Central Trains work to Peterborough and beyond.

After crossing the water meadows west of Trowse Lower Junction with the Ipswich line, this route follows an easily graded course via former junctions at Wymondham, Roudham and Thetford before looping through the conifers of Thetford Chase to Brandon and the Fens beyond. It used also to carry Norwich-Dereham line services and trains between Thetford and Swaffham.

Norwich-Diss (Ipswich)

Stations: Trowse (1m), Swainsthorpe (5.25m), Flordon (8.25m), Forncett (11m), Tivetshall (14.5m), Burston (17.5m), Diss (20m).

Opening and closure: An Ipswich & Bury Railway project taken over by the Eastern Union Railway with opening northwards to Burston on 8.7.1849 and to Norwich Victoria in December 1849; link to Thorpe 1851. Victoria closed to passengers 22.5.1916, Swainsthorpe 5.7.1954, others stations except Diss 7.11.1966. Goods closures 1964-66.

Route and traffic: From Thorpe station, the Wensum swing bridge and Trowse Lower Junction, the double-track Great Eastern main line, now electrified, rises to a high viaduct over the River Yare and the Ely line, then heads south along the valley of the River Tas. It once carried Beccles trains as well as those to London, but today the Great Eastern electrified services hurry past the former junctions at Forncett and Tivetshall – where steam trains used the water troughs – to make Diss the first call on their 109-minute run to London (once 255 minutes by stopping train). Freight on the route included coal, agricultural machinery, fuel oil, fertilisers and grain traffic at Diss.

Norwich-Kings Lynn

Stations: Trowse (1m), Hethersett (6.25m), Wymondham (10.25m), Kimberley Park (14m), Hardingham (15.75m), Thuxton (17.25m), Yaxham (19.75m), Dereham (21.75m), Wendling (25.75m), Fransham (28.5m), Dunham (29.75m), Swaffham (33.75m), Narborough & Pentney (39.5m), East Winch (43m), Middleton Towers (45m).

Opening and closure: The Norfolk Railway opened Wymondham-Dereham for freight 7.12.1846 and for passengers 15.2.1847. The Lynn & Dereham Railway opened from the north end 27.10.1846 to 11.9.1848. Connecting spur 1884. Passenger services ended between Lynn and Dereham on 9.9.1968 and between Dereham and Norwich on 6.10.1969. The southern section survived for bulk grain and is now the subject of a preservation scheme by the Mid-Norfolk Railway.

Route and traffic: This pleasant mid-Norfolk railway was double track to Dereham (until 13.6.1965), then single with five passing loops. It was the province of high-stepping 'Claud Hamilton' 4-4-0s hurrying with the Tuesday express to Lynn or an all-stations Wells service with its Lynn connection engined by Dereham. Freight came mainly from Dereham (grain, engineering, furniture, etc), which, like Swaffham, had several private sidings. At the Kings Lynn end supplies for RAF Marham used Narborough station, and sand from Middleton Towers kept a section of the route in use after general closure.

Norwich-Lowestoft

Stations: Whitlingham (1.75m), Brundall Gardens Halt (4.75m), Brundall (5.75m), Buckenham (7.75m), Cantley (10m), Reedham (12.25m), Haddiscoe (16.25m), Somerleyton (18m), Oulton Broad North (22m).

Opening and closure: Norwich-Reedham section opened by the Yarmouth & Norwich Railway 1.5.1844, Reedham-Lowestoft by the Lowestoft Railway & Harbour to goods 3.5.1847 and passengers 1.7.1847. Brundall Gardens Halt opened 1924. Whitlingham closed to passengers 19.9.1955 and local goods facilities withdrawn in 1964.

Route and traffic: This level, 23.5-mile double line crosses the Yare twice before Whitlingham Junction and remains close to the river through the Brundall boatyards and junction and on to Reedham where a swing bridge crossing follows the junction for Yarmouth. After the next stretch along the New Cut there were spurs to the East Suffolk line at Haddiscoe before the crossing of Somerleyton's swing bridge and the final Lowestoft entry via Oulton Broad and Lake Lothing. Anglia Railways local trains via Brundall and via Reedham maintain the line's tradition of high passenger utilisation, although the through services to Leeds, Newcastle and Southport have long gone. The main freight movement was sugar beet to the Cantley factory plus fish vans from Yarmouth and Lowestoft.

Norwich-Sheringham

Stations: Whitlingham (2m), Salhouse (6m), Wroxham (8.75m), Worstead (13m), North Walsham (16m), Gunton (19.75m), Cromer (24m), West Runton (26.75m).

Opening and closure: Opened by the East Norfolk Railway from Whitlingham Junction to North Walsham 20.10.1874, to Gunton 29.7.1876 and to Cromer 26.3.1877. Link to 16.1.1887 line to Sheringham 23.7.1906. Whitlingham closed 19.9.1955 (passengers) and 13.7.1964 (goods). Cromer High closed to passengers 20.9.1954 and to goods 7.3.1960.

Route and traffic: Now carrying an Anglia Railways local service, this was once the 28.5-mile route of trains like the 'Norfolk Coast Express', 'Norfolkman', 'Broadsman' and 'East Anglian'. Restaurant Car expresses from Liverpool Street followed the double-track section to North Walsham with the Cromer and Sheringham portions then going forward over the rising single line to the route dividing point at Cromer Junction. Many Broads visitors still use Wroxham station, but the Norwich-Dereham and Mundesley line services have long gone. Singling in the 1960s included the Wroxham-North Walsham section and a new, simplified station was used at Sheringham from 1967.

Norwich-Yarmouth

Stations: Whitlingham (2m), Brundall Gardens Halt (4.75m), Brundall (5.75m), Lingwood (8m), Acle (10.5m).

Opening and closure: Opened Yarmouth to Acle by the Eastern Counties Railway 12.3.1883 and on to Brundall 1.6.1883. Whitlingham closed to passengers 19.9.1955, goods closures 1964-69.

Route and traffic: This 11m 2ch cut-off line from Brundall to the coast has a passing loop at Acle before the bleak, flat crossing of Acle Marshes where hundreds of Irish cattle were once brought for fattening. Day-tripper traffic has always been quite considerable and evening excursion tickets were once big business. The line became the main rail route to Yarmouth after the closure of South Town and still carries over 30 Anglia Railways trains each day.

Reedham-Yarmouth

Station: Berney Arms (3.5m).

Opening: By the Yarmouth & Norwich Railway 1.5.1844.

Route and traffic: Boldly going where no roads

go, this 7-mile single line heads across Reedham Marshes to the tiny platform at Berney Arms, then along the edge of Breydon Water to Breydon Junction and Yarmouth Vauxhall. Closure of Berney Arms was attempted in 1850 and again a century later, but this remote pioneer line still has four daily Anglia Railways services.

Stoke Ferry branch

Stations: Denver (1.5m), Ryston (3m), Abbey (5.5m), Stoke Ferry (8.75m).

Opening and closure: Opened 1.8.1882 as the Downham & Stoke Ferry Light Railway operated by the GER. Closed to passengers 22.9.1930, to freight 1964-66.

Route and traffic: This single-line branch left the Kings Lynn-Ely main line at Denver Junction and ran 7m 9ch east to a single-platform terminus at Stoke Ferry. A single set of coaches provided four daily workings starting from Stoke Ferry at 8.30am and ending there at 6.20pm. From 1925 the line was busy in the sugar beet season with inwards movements to the Wissington factory. Abbey station provided a connection with the Wissington Light Railway, a network of agricultural lines opened on 30.11.1905 and worked by the LNER for the BSC and the Ministry of Agriculture. It closed in 1957.

Thetford-Swaffham

Stations: Wretham & Hockham (6.5m), Stow Bedon (10.25m), Watton (13m), Holme Hale (18.5m).

Opening and closure: Thetford & Watton Railway opened 26.1.1869 for freight and 18.10.1869 for passengers; Watton & Swaffham Railway opened 20.9.1875 and 15.11.1875 respectively. Closed to passengers 15.6.1964, to freight 19.4.1965.

Route and traffic: This lonely single line began at Roudham Junction, 4m 15ch east of Thetford, and ran northwards for 18m 32ch via a passing loop at Watton. The 7.36am from Swaffham ran five daily trips each way to finish back there 14 hours later. Coal, poultry, sugar beet and RAF traffic were the main freight movements.

Tivetshall-Beccles

Stations: Pulham Market (2.75m), Pulham St Mary (3.75m), Harleston (6.25m), Homersfield (9m), Earsham (12m), Bungay (13m), Ditchingham (13.75m), Ellingham (15.25m), Geldeston (16.75m).

Opening and closure: Opened eastwards to Harleston by the Waveney Valley Railway 1.12.1855, to Bungay 2.11.1860 and to Beccles 2.3.1863. Some early station closures with final passenger closure 5.1.1953 and freight 1.2.1960 to 18.4.1966.

Route and traffic: This 19.5-mile single line with passing loops at Harleston and Bungay carried a weekday Norwich-Beccles service of seven trains each way. The gentle route along the valley of the infant River Waveney also handled coal, beet, agricultural traffic, implements and wartime supplies for several RAF stations. Final operation was as a freight light railway with the centre section closed.

Wisbech

The original 1847 line from March to a site by the River Nene has continued in use for freight long after the closure of Wisbech East and the link on to Magdalen Road and Kings Lynn or that of the 1866-1959 M&GN line on the west side of the river. The latter had a branch trailing back to the harbour and the former a harbour branch, a small loco shed, timber and cannery sidings, and the 5m 74ch roadside tramway through the fruit-growing areas to Upwell.

Wisbech-Magdalen Road

Stations: Emneth (2.5m), Smeeth Road (3.75m), Middle Drove (5.25m).

Opening and closure: Opened by the East Anglian Railway 1.2.1848. Closed to freight 19.4.1965, completely 9.9.1968.

Route and traffic: This 9m 44ch Fenland single line involved crossings of the Wisbech Canal, the Middle Level Drain and, on the approach to Magdalen Road, the Old and New Bedford Rivers. High construction costs and isolated stations gave the route a poor start, but it came to carry a useful March-Kings Lynn service of 24 trains a day, including several running fast between Wisbech and Kings Lynn.

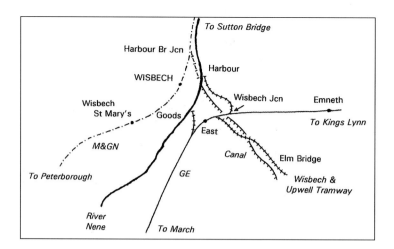

Wisbech & Upwell Tramway

Stations: Elm Bridge (1.75m), Boyce's Bridge (3.25m), Outwell Basin (4m), Outwell (5m), Upwell (6m).

Opening and closure: Opened by the GER to Outwell 20.8.1883 and to Upwell 8.9.1884. Closed to passengers 2.1.1928, to freight 23.5.1966.

Route and traffic: This single-line, 5m 74ch roadside tramway ran beside the Wisbech Canal and the A1101 road to Outwell, then on to a terminus at Upwell. Special coaches were provided for the service of 12 daily passenger trains, and LNER Class 'J70' 0-6-0 tram engines with enclosed motion worked the services until Drewry diesels took over in 1952. Clerical staff travelled with a special office van to waybill the heavy seasonal fruit forwardings.

Wroxham-County School

Stations: Coltishall (2.75m), Buxton Lamas (5.5m), Aylsham (9m), Cawston (13.25m), Reepham (15.25m), Foulsham (20m).

Opening and closure: Opened westward in stages by the East Norfolk Railway from 8.7.1879 to 1.5.1882. Closed to passengers 15.9.1952, but eastern end retained for Lenwade buildings traffic by construction of new Themelthorpe Curve from Reepham 12.9.1960. Final closure 1982.

Route and traffic: This 23.75-mile single line with passing loops at Aylsham and Reepham was so rural that it was nicknamed 'Round the

World'. The 15 daily trains (summer 1938) took around 85 minutes for the 38.5-mile Norwich-Dereham journey, and there was a through Yarmouth train on some summer Sundays. Coal, sugar beet and supplies for RAF Coltishall were the main freight traffics. The Wroxham-Aylsham trackbed now accommodates the 15-inch-gauge line of the Bure Valley Railway.

Yarmouth

Yarmouth Vauxhall originated with the Yarmouth & Norwich Railway in 1844, Yarmouth South Town followed in 1859, and Yarmouth Beach (M&GN) in 1877. The importance of the fishing industry was recognised as early as 1847 when a tramway was constructed along North Quay to the fish market. Beach was connected to the street tramway in 1882 and, via Breydon Water and a swing bridge, to the 1903 Norfolk & Suffolk line from South Town to Lowestoft. Today Anglia Railways trains link Norwich with the surviving Vauxhall station.

Yarmouth-Beccles

Stations: Belton & Burgh (4m), St Olaves (6.5m), Haddiscoe (7m), Aldeby (9.25m).

Opening and closure: Beccles-Haddiscoe opened 20.11.1854 for goods and 4.12.1854 for passengers by the Halesworth, Beccles & Haddiscoe Railway. Extended to Yarmouth South Town 1.6.1859 by the East Suffolk Railway. Closed 2.11.1959.

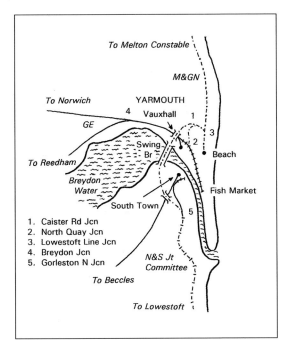

Route and traffic: This was the former 12m 41ch double-track main line from Yarmouth South Town to Beccles and on to Liverpool Street, carrying both fast trains and locals, some with Lowestoft portions added or detached at Beccles. The level route crossed the River Waveney by a swing bridge near the high-level station at Haddiscoe and again before the three-way North Junction at Beccles. Two spurs linked the Lowestoft and Beccles lines at Haddiscoe (once Herringfleet exchange station), another surviving for sugar beet from Aldeby until 1965.

Midland & Great Northern Joint Railway

Consisting of the lines from Peterborough and Saxby via South Lynn to Norwich, Cromer and Yarmouth, the M&GN was owned jointly by the Midland and the Great Northern companies. It was formed on 1.7.1893 from the Eastern & Midlands Railway, itself a 1.1.1883 amalgam of Midland & Eastern, Peterborough, Wisbech & Sutton Bridge, Lynn & Fakenham, Yarmouth & North Norfolk and Yarmouth Union companies. It was worked jointly under a Traffic Manager at Kings Lynn until the LNER took over the working from 1.10.1936. Most of the 182m 32ch system was closed on 2.3.1959.

Kings Lynn-Sutton Bridge

Stations: South Lynn (2m), Clenchwarton (5m), Terrington (6.25m), Walpole (8.5m).
Opening and closure: The Lynn & Sutton Bridge Railway opened this section on 1.11.1864 after the Norwich & Spalding had arrived at Sutton Bridge on 1.7.1862 and before the Peterborough, Wisbech & Sutton Bridge opened on 1.8.1866. Closure was on 2.3.1959.
Route and traffic: From West Lynn this line was double track all the way to the swing bridge over the Nene at the county boundary and preceding Sutton Bridge station and the junction between the Peterborough and Spalding lines. That junction brought semi-fast and local trains from the former and through trains from Manchester, Leicester, Derby and Nottingham via Saxby and Bourne. The single-line section over the bridge, now converted to road use, was a major train operator's headache on busy summer Saturdays. Substantial agricultural traffic passed over the route.

Kings Lynn-Yarmouth

Stations: South Lynn (2m), Gayton Road (5.5m), Grimston Road (8.25m), Hillingdon (10.25m), Massingham (15m), East Rudham (18.25m), Raynham Park (20m), Fakenham West (24m), Thursford (30.25m), Melton Constable (33.5m), Corpusty & Saxthorpe (38.25m), Aylsham (45m), Felmingham (48.25m), North Walsham (50.5m), Honing (53.5m), Stalham (57.25m), Catfield (59.5m), Potter Heigham (62.25m), Martham (65m), Hemsby (67.75m), Great Ormesby (69.5m), Caister-on-Sea (72.25m).
Opening and closure: The Yarmouth & North Norfolk Railway opened to North Walsham progressively 7.8.1877 to 13.6.1881, Kings Lynn to Melton Constable by the Lynn & Fakenham Railway 16.8.1879 to 19.1.1882, and Melton Constable to North Walsham by the Eastern & Midlands 5.4.1883. System closed 2.3.1959.

Route and traffic: The 75-mile route across North Norfolk and down the coast was single with passing loops from Grimston Road to Raynham Park and from Corpusty to Yarmouth. Stopping trains took 3 hours, 'expresses' from the Midlands only slightly less. The route served the Norfolk Broads and had seaside halts on the section north of Yarmouth Beach, but off-peak business, both passenger and freight, was never more than modest.

Melton Constable

Lying 31m 43ch from South Lynn, Melton Constable station was preceded by the meeting of the Lynn and Cromer lines at West Junction and followed by the separation of the Norwich and Yarmouth lines at East Junction. Reached by the Lynn & Fakenham Railway on 19.1.1882, Melton Constable grew into a sizeable railway town with locomotive and rolling-stock works and a busy running shed (32G) with a 70-foot turntable.

Melton Constable-Cromer

Stations: Holt (5m), Weybourne (8.5m), Sheringham (11.25m), West Runton (13m).

Opening and closure: Melton Constable to Holt opened by Eastern & Midlands Railway 1.10.1884, and Holt to Cromer 16.1.1887. Melton Constable-Sheringham closed to passengers 6.4.1964, to goods 28.12.1964. Sheringham-Holt reopened progressively by the North Norfolk Railway.

Route and traffic: This 15-mile single line had passing loops at Holt, Weybourne and Sheringham, and 1 in 80 sections at the western end. Over the years the passenger train service varied from 10 to 30 trains daily, with through services to Kings Cross, the Midlands, Liverpool Street and Yarmouth via Mundesley also featuring. The line carried military traffic to and from Weybourne and Holt, Norfolk CC had a siding at the latter point, and there was a locomotive sub-shed with turntable at Cromer.

Anglia Railways train services operate between Sheringham and Norwich from a simple 1967 station at Sheringham, the adjacent original station now being the

headquarters of the North Norfolk Railway's preservation activities.

Melton Constable-Norwich

Stations: Hindolvestone (2m), Guestwick (4.5m), Whitwell & Reepham (8.5m), Lenwade (10.75m), Attlebridge (12.5m), Drayton (16.75m), Hellesdon (19.25m).

Opening and closure: Melton Constable-Guestwick opened by the Lynn & Fakenham Railway 19.1.1882, on to Lenwade 1.7.1882 and to Norwich 2.12.1882. Closed to passengers 2.3.1959 and section north of Themelthorpe closed completely when route linked to former GER Aylsham line. Lenwade-Norwich City closed 3.2.1969.

Route and traffic: This 21.25-mile single line followed a pleasant, level course to approach Norwich via the valley of the River Wensum. There were passing loops at Whitwell and Drayton to cater for some 20 passenger trains a day with extras on market days and Saturdays. In later years there was a coal concentration depot as well as a small loco depot at Norwich City, and a major flow of prefabricated buildings via the Themelthorpe Curve. Norwich City station was destroyed in a wartime bombing raid and rebuilt in a very utilitarian form.

Norfolk & Suffolk Joint Committee

The Committee was established in 1897 as a vehicle for co-operation between the M&GN Joint and Great Eastern railways in the Norfolk seaside areas. It was confirmed by an Act of 27.7.1898 and had eight directors, four GER, two GNR and two from the Midland Railway

Lowestoft-Yarmouth

Stations: Lowestoft North (2.25m), Corton (3.75m), Hopton (5.75m), Gorleston-on-Sea (7.75m), Gorleston North (9m).

Opening and closure: Opened 13.7.1903 after Lowestoft Central-Yarmouth South Town was authorised to the GER and link to Yarmouth

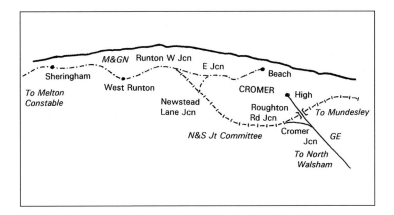

Beach to the M&GN (as Lowestoft Junction Railway), but vested in the N&S Joint Committee on formation. Closure of Gorleston North 5.10.1942 after bomb damage, Breydon section closed to passengers 21.9.1953; remainder 4.5.1970.

Route and traffic: After leaving the Lowestoft-Beccles/Reedham line at Coke Ovens Junction, the double-track N&S route turned north to follow a fairly level course along the coast to Gorleston and Yarmouth South Town (10.25m). From Gorleston North Junction a 2m 11ch M&GN line to Yarmouth Beach (12.25m) crossed the 800-foot single-track swing bridge over Breydon Water and a smaller bridge over the GER line and the River Bure. In its best periods the line had over 20 passenger trains each way daily in summer running to Beach and South Town alternately, and in the 1950s Gorleston had its own holiday camp special, but winter business and general freight was never more than modest. Gorleston Links Halt was located north of Hopton.

North Walsham-Cromer

Stations: Paston & Knapton (3.5m), Mundesley-on-Sea (5.5m), Trimingham (7.75m), Overstrand (10.25m), Golf Links Halt (11m).

Opening and closure: North Walsham to Mundesley opened by the M&GN to freight 20.6.1898 and to passengers 1.7.1898. Extension to Cromer by the N&S Joint Committee followed on 3.8.1906 (freight March 1907) after a Cromer Junction to West Runton Junction link had permitted GER access to Sheringham from 23.7.1906. Closed Mundesley to Cromer 7.4.1953, North Walsham to Mundesley 5.10.1964 (passengers), 28.12.1964 (freight).

Route and traffic: For a Norfolk byway this 14.5-mile single line was quite steeply graded and had a succession of cuttings and embankments to ease them to an average of 1 in 100. It carried a reasonable train service, mainly from the GER station at North Walsham and with some trains terminating at Mundesley, but, apart from the peak summer months, loadings were never heavy – this was another line built to stimulate 'resorts' that never quite lived up to expectations. Mundesley had a passing loop and camping coaches. Halts were opened at Cromer Links in 1923 and at Sidestrand in 1936.

INDEX OF LOCATIONS